AGILE IS A

MINDSET

...Not a Methodology!

A Foundational Guide to Agile

PHILL AKINWALE, CSM, PSM, PSPO, PAL, SPS, PMI-ACP, PMP

PraizionMedia

Real World Project Management Training Solutions

Agile is a Mindset
Published by Praizion Media
P.O Box 22241, Mesa, AZ 85277
E-mail: info@praizion.com
www.praizion.com

Author:
Phillip Akinwale, MSc, OPM3, PMP, PMI-ACP, PSM, CSM, SPS, PAL

ISBN 978-1-934579-20-6

9 781934 579206

CONTENTS

CHAPTER ONE: INTRODUCTION

As a leader in his firm, Billy Brag, a renowned leader in the tech industry, often found himself at the center of discussion when it came to Agile.

People revered him for his use of Scrum and Kanban frameworks, considering him the epitome of Agile. However, deep down, Billy knew something was missing. Despite his team's "ok" deliveries, he felt an unshakeable sense of dissatisfaction. He couldn't help but feel that they were missing the essence of being truly Agile. One day, while attending a tech conference, Billy had a chance encounter with an old sage Pip, renowned for his expertise in Agile. The sage, intrigued by Billy's reputation, asked him about his approach to Agile. As Billy described his practices, the sage gently smiled, seeing Billy's misconception.

Pip the sage explained that Agile was not merely about using Scrum or Kanban, or any other framework or methodology for that matter. He described Agile as a mindset, a way of thinking that shapes one's attitude, behaviors, and actions. This mindset was about adaptability, growth, inquisitiveness, continuous learning, and evolution. The sage highlighted that true Agility required embracing change, fostering collaboration, prioritizing customer value, and striving for continuous improvement.

Agile is not a project management methodology or a methodology or a framework. It is a mindset—a mental attitude and set of beliefs that shape one's thoughts, behaviors, and actions. This book aims to clarify the true nature of agile and its significance in responding to the ever-changing world.

In today's tech-driven society, the topic of agile was explored with the help of Chat GPT and Bard. However, their responses failed to capture the essence of agile, perpetuating misconceptions about its nature. It is crucial to understand that agile is not a methodology, framework, or project management approach. Agile is a mindset that enables individuals and teams to adapt to the rapidly changing world around them.

Understanding Agile

Agile, a term widely used (often incorrectly) in the realm of project management, often gets misunderstood. Agile is neither a methodology nor a specific framework; it is, in essence, a mindset. This mindset is embodied in the Agile Manifesto, a revolutionary document crafted by 17 professionals I consider to be pioneers in 2001. It presented a fresh perspective on tackling product development and complex problems, prioritizing individuals and interactions over processes and tools, working products over comprehensive documentation, customer collaboration over contract negotiation, and responding to change over following a plan.

Understanding the Agile Manifesto

To delve deeper into the agile mindset, let's examine the Agile Manifesto, which encapsulates the values and principles of agile thinking. The Agile Manifesto emphasizes the following key values:

Agile Manifesto Values

i.   Individuals and interactions over processes and tools: Value the importance of human connections and collaboration within a project, prioritizing individuals over rigid processes or tools.

ii. Working software over comprehensive documentation: Emphasize the practical implementation of functional software rather than excessive documentation, enabling faster feedback and progress.

iii. Customer collaboration over contract negotiation: Foster a collaborative relationship with customers, involving them throughout the product development process to ensure their needs are met.

iv. Responding to change over following a plan: Be open to change and adaptable in response to evolving requirements, placing a higher value on flexibility than strict adherence to initial plans.

By embracing and valuing these values, one can begin to adopt an agile mindset and approach to work. Agile is not a static state achieved overnight but rather an ongoing journey of continuous improvement and adaptation.

Agile Manifesto Principles

These principles embody the core values of customer satisfaction, adaptability, collaboration, and continuous improvement. By embracing these principles, Agile teams are able to deliver value to customers more effectively, foster collaboration and innovation, and create a culture of learning and flexibility.

Let's explore these principles and understand how they contribute to the success of Agile projects.

1. Customer satisfaction: Our top priority is to satisfy the customer by continuously delivering valuable software, adapting to their changing needs, and seeking their feedback to ensure their satisfaction.

2. Embracing change: We welcome changing requirements and see them as opportunities for innovation and improvement, allowing us to stay ahead in the ever-changing market.

3. Continuous delivery: We strive to deliver working software frequently, embracing shorter timescales, collaborating with customers, and gathering feedback to ensure we meet their expectations.

4. Collaborative environment: Business people and developers work closely together on a daily basis, fostering trust, open communication, and shared understanding to achieve project success.

5. Motivated individuals: We provide an environment that supports and empowers individuals, encouraging self-organization, creativity, and ownership to drive project success.

6. Effective communication: Face-to-face communication is our preferred method for

conveying information, as it enables immediate feedback, promotes understanding, and strengthens collaboration.

7. Working software as a measure: Working software is our primary measure of progress, reflecting our focus on continuous development, testing, and delivery to maintain a sustainable pace and ensure quality.

8. Sustainable development: We value sustainable development practices that prioritize the well-being of the team, avoiding burnout and technical debt, to ensure long-term success.

9. Technical excellence: We strive for continuous attention to technical excellence and good design, emphasizing regular refactoring, testing, and adapting to emerging technologies and practices.

10. Simplicity and efficiency: We emphasize simplicity and aim to maximize value by focusing on essential features, eliminating unnecessary complexity, and delivering efficiently.

11. Self-organizing teams: We trust and empower self-organizing teams, allowing them to make decisions,

collaborate, and adapt based on their expertise to produce the best outcomes.

12. Continuous improvement: We regularly reflect on our work, seeking opportunities for improvement, learning from experience, and adapting our approach to continually maximize value and quality.

In conclusion, Agile is more than just a buzzword and it is not a methodology. It is a mindset, a way of thinking and working that emphasizes adaptability, collaboration, and continuous improvement. The 12 principles of Agile serve as guiding pillars for teams to follow, allowing them to embrace change, prioritize customer satisfaction, and deliver value in a fast-paced and unpredictable environment.

By adopting the Agile principles, teams can break away from traditional, rigid approaches and instead focus on flexibility, communication, and self-organization. The iterative nature of Agile allows for regular feedback, learning, and adaptation, enabling teams to respond quickly to customer needs and market dynamics.

Agile is not a one-size-fits-all solution, and it requires a shift in mindset and a commitment to continuous learning. It encourages collaboration, transparency, and a focus on delivering incremental value. Agile empowers teams to take ownership, make decisions, and continuously improve their processes and outcomes.

While Agile principles are often applied in software development, their concepts and benefits extend beyond the IT industry. Agile can be embraced in various domains where adaptability, collaboration, and responsiveness are valued.

In a world that is constantly evolving, Agile provides a mindset for organizations to navigate uncertainty, seize opportunities, and stay ahead of the competition. By embracing the Agile mindset and its guiding principles, teams can foster a culture of innovation, customer-centricity, and continuous growth.

Remember, Agile is not a destination but a journey—an ongoing pursuit of excellence and agility. It requires commitment, open-mindedness, and a willingness to challenge the status quo. Embracing Agile can lead to transformative outcomes and enable organizations to thrive in today's dynamic and ever-changing landscape. Agile develops DAILY not in a day!

CHAPTER TWO: AGILE MINDSET MANTRA

M oving on in our story about Billy, One day, during a workshop, Pip pulled Billy aside.

They found a quiet spot in the auditorium, away from the noise and activity of the main workshop. It was here that Pip dropped a truth bomb on Billy, "Agile isn't about using Scrum or Kanban, Billy. It's about a mindset, a way of thinking. It's about embracing change, fostering growth, and fostering a spirit of continuous learning."

The statement stunned Billy, forcing him to rethink everything he thought he knew about Agile. As he grappled with this new understanding, Pip offered him a mantra, something to guide him on his journey towards embracing the true Agile mindset.

"Adapt, Grow, Innovate, Learn, and Evolve", Pip said, his voice steady and calm, "That's the Agile mindset. It's not just about implementing Scrum and Kanban, it's about being ready to adapt to changing circumstances, being eager to grow, always looking for innovative solutions, and being willing to learn from mistakes and evolve."

The Mindset Mantra

To understand agile, it's essential to distinguish between a growth mindset and a fixed mindset. A growth mindset is characterized by the belief that abilities and intelligence can be developed through effort, learning, and persistence. On the other hand, a fixed mindset believes that abilities and intelligence are fixed traits and cannot be significantly changed.

Agile is about embracing a growth mindset and being

open to learning about new approaches and ideas. It is not about sticking to preconceived notions or being resistant to change. Agility requires the willingness to pivot and adapt when necessary, as the world around us is constantly evolving. As Jack Welch said, "Change before you have to."

The examples of Toys R Us and Blockbuster illustrate the consequences of not being agile. These companies failed to adapt to changing market trends and technologies, leading to their downfall. Agile is about being adaptable, responsive, and quick to embrace new opportunities.

The acronym **A.G.I.L.E**. further helps in understanding what agilility is:

A stands for adaptability: Being flexible and finding different ways to handle challenges.
G stands for growth: Focusing on personal and continuous growth, as well as using empiricism to inform decisions.
I stands for inquisitiveness and innovation: Asking

questions, reflecting on improvements, and exploring new ideas.

L stands for learning: Having a mindset of continuous learning and expanding understanding.

E stands for evolving: Viewing agility as an evolution, continuously changing and improving over time.

It's also important to clarify what agile is not.

Agile is not limited to specific frameworks, principles, or frameworks like Scrum or Kanban. It cannot be forced upon people, and it is not a one-size-fits-all solution. Agile does not disregard the value of long-term planning or strategic goals. It does not allow for the avoidance of accountability or responsibility. Agile is not solely focused on individual tasks or activities; it emphasizes collaboration, teamwork, and customer-centricity. It also requires clear communication, effective leadership, and a commitment to quality.

In summary, agile is an active, dynamic, and ever-evolving mindset that emphasizes adaptability, growth, inquisitiveness, learning, and efficiency. It encourages continuous improvement, teamwork, and finding joy in what you do.

Agility is not limited to the business context but can be applied to personal growth as well. It's about being determined to chase success and always striving to build a better mousetrap.

Implementing Agile in Practice

Now that we have a solid understanding of the agile manifesto and the agile mindset, let's explore how agile principles can be implemented in real-world scenarios.

Agile implementation involves adopting agile practices, fostering collaboration, and embracing an iterative and incremental approach to work. Practices of agile include:

1. Iterative Development: Agile promotes an iterative approach, where work is divided into small, manageable segments called iterations or sprints. Each iteration involves planning, executing, reviewing, and adapting based on feedback. This

iterative development cycle allows for incremental value delivery, continuous learning, and the ability to respond to changing requirements.

2. Incremental Delivery: Agile promotes breaking down work into smaller, manageable increments that can be completed within short time frames (time boxes called iterations). This iterative approach allows for faster feedback, increased transparency, and the ability to adapt and adjust as needed.

3. Embracing Change: Agile teams understand that change is inevitable and welcome it as an opportunity for improvement. Instead of rigidly adhering to initial plans, agile practitioners embrace change by continuously reassessing priorities, incorporating feedback, and adjusting their approach.

4. Cross-Functional Collaboration: Agile encourages close collaboration between team members, stakeholders, and customers throughout the development process. By fostering effective communication, shared ownership, and collective

decision-making, agile teams can leverage diverse perspectives and ensure that the end product meets customer needs.

5. Continuous Improvement: Agility is not a destination but a journey of constant improvement. Agile teams regularly reflect on their work, identify areas for enhancement, and implement changes to enhance efficiency, productivity, and quality.

6. Rapid Feedback: Agile teams prioritize obtaining feedback early and frequently throughout the development process. This feedback loop helps to validate assumptions, identify areas for improvement, and ensure alignment with customer needs. By incorporating feedback promptly, teams can make necessary adjustments and deliver higher-quality outcomes.

7. Continuous Integration: Agile teams practice continuous integration, which involves integrating code changes frequently and regularly. This practice helps identify and resolve integration issues early on, promoting collaboration and

maintaining a working product at all times. By continuously integrating previously completed work, teams can minimize conflicts and deliver reliable, stable products.

8. Collaborative Work: Agile emphasizes collaboration and cross-functional teamwork. Instead of working in silos, team members with different skills and expertise collaborate closely throughout the project. This practice fosters better communication, knowledge sharing, and a collective ownership mindset, leading to increased productivity and better outcomes.

9. Timeboxing: Agile teams employ timeboxing, a technique where specific time frames are allocated for various activities or tasks. Timeboxing ensures that work is scoped and bounded, preventing over-commitment and enabling better planning. It also promotes discipline and helps teams focus on delivering the most valuable features within set time constraints.

Kaizen

Kaizen is a practice deeply rooted in the Agile mindset and is derived from the Japanese philosophy of continuous improvement. In Agile, Kaizen emphasizes the relentless pursuit of improvement in all aspects of work. It is not limited to specific processes or methodologies but extends to every individual, team, and organization.

The essence of Kaizen lies in the belief that even small, incremental changes can lead to significant improvements over time. It encourages individuals and teams to regularly evaluate their work, identify areas for enhancement, and take deliberate actions to make those improvements. Kaizen fosters a culture of learning, adaptability, and self-reflection. In an Agile context, Kaizen is about making small improvements throughout the development process. It encourages teams to experiment, learn from failures, and leverage successes to continuously refine their practices. It involves asking questions like "How can we do this better?" or "What can we learn from this experience?" and taking proactive steps to implement the answers.

Kaizen also promotes the notion that improvement is a collective effort. It encourages collaboration, open communication, and the sharing of insights and ideas among team members. Everyone is empowered to contribute to the improvement process, regardless of their role or level of expertise.

By embracing Kaizen, Agile teams create a culture of continuous learning and growth. They become more adaptable to change, more responsive to customer needs, and more efficient in delivering value. Kaizen helps teams identify and eliminate waste, optimize processes, and ultimately achieve higher levels of quality and productivity.

CHAPTER THREE: DEEPER INTO SCRUM

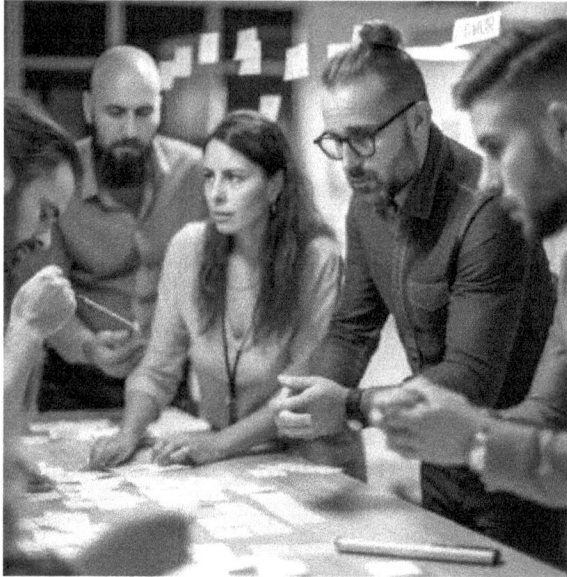

Moving on to **Chapter 3**, The sage's words hit Billy like a lightning bolt. Agile wasn't about a set of practices or tools but a way of life. It wasn't a fixed or innate quality but a flexible, adaptable aspect of cognition. Armed with this newfound understanding, Billy decided it was time to bring about change. He realized that for his team to be truly Agile, they needed to adopt this mindset.

Back at his company, Billy embarked on the journey of transforming his team. He shared his insights from the encounter with the sage and stressed the importance of the Agile mindset. They started to see Agile as more than Scrum and Kanban. They began to question their methods and processes, striving for continuous improvement and growth. The team began an introspective look at why Scrum was the way it was, looking for a greater meaning to how they executed work.

Now, let's shift our focus to Scrum, the most popular Agile-based framework (used by millions) that promotes a collaborative and iterative approach to project development. A Scrum Team includes three roles: the Product Owner, the Scrum Master, and the Developers (or Development Team).

Product Owner

The Product Owner serves as the liaison between the stakeholders and the team, ensuring the product backlog is refined and prioritized.

Scrum Master

The Scrum Master coaches the team in the Scrum practices, resolves obstacles, and ensures Scrum is being implemented effectively.

Developers

The Developers or Development Team consists of professionals who carry out the work to deliver potentially releasable increments of the product.

The Scrum Team

The Scrum Team consists of all three key roles: the Product Owner, the Scrum Master, and the Developers. Together, they form a cohesive unit dedicated to delivering high-quality products through the principles and practices of Scrum. The Product Owner serves as the bridge between the stakeholders and the team, representing the interests of the customers and users.

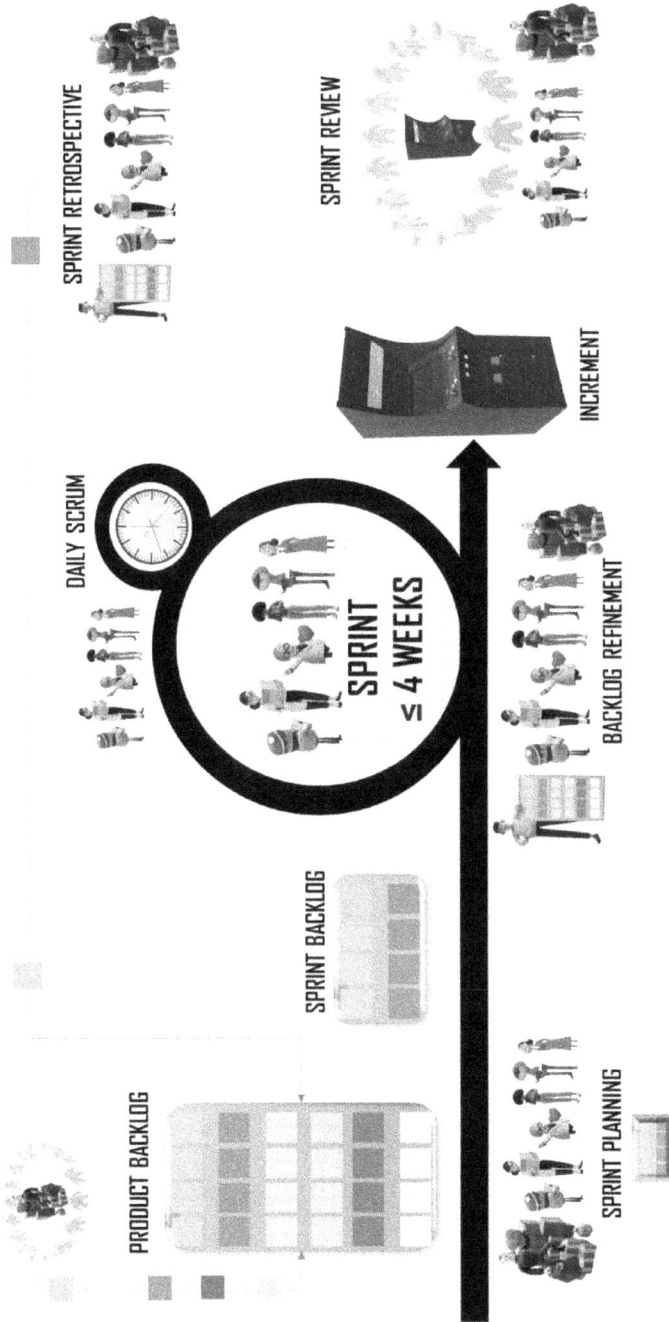

Figure 1: The Scrum Framework

The Vitality of User Stories

In Agile and Scrum, User Stories play a crucial role. They capture product functionality from the user's perspective, defining who the user is, what they need, and why. They are not obligatory in Scrum but several teams use them due to their effectiveness.

An effective User Story is framed within the role-goal-benefit context, outlining not only the user's role and intent but also the value they seek. For instance, "As a customer, I want to create a profile so that I don't have to fill in the information again when I make a purchase." This User Story emphasizes the customer's desire for convenience in making repeated purchases.

In contrast, a poorly articulated User Story fails to express the user's underlying value. Take, for instance, "As a customer, I want to create a profile so that I can have an account." The lack of expressed value makes this User Story vague and inadequate.

Exploring More User Story Examples

To foster a more comprehensive understanding of User Stories, let's explore some examples provided by Agile guru, Mike Cohn.

"As a club member, I can search for profiles based on a few fields so I can find people I know or might want to connect with."

"As a site member, I can mark my information and email address as private, even if the rest of my profile is not, so that no one can contact me without my consent."

These examples vividly illustrate the role-goal-benefit framework for story-writing, making them strong User Stories. However, bear in mind that User Stories are not obligatory in Scrum. They are tools to facilitate communication and understanding of the user's needs.

The Daily Scrum

Moving on to another integral part of the Scrum framework: the Daily Scrum. This daily event provides an opportunity for the development team to sync on the progress towards the Sprint goal. Three typical questions form the foundation of this meeting:

   i.   What did you do yesterday to move us towards our Sprint goal?

   ii.   What are you going to do today to move us towards the Sprint goal?

  iii.   Are there any impediments in your way?

The Role of the Scrum Master

The Scrum Master's role emerges significantly during these events. Their goal is to first of all, ensure these meetings hold and are productive and then, ensure that the team understands Scrum. They are accountable to implement and coach the team in practicing Scrum effectively. They are also responsible for addressing any impediments that may block the team's progress.

Walking the Board with Kanban

A noteworthy technique used in daily Scrum meetings is "walking the board," often implemented using a Kanban board. Originating from Kanban, a Kanban board visualizes work, allowing the team to see the status of different tasks or stories.

A simple Kanban board consists of three columns: To-Do, Doing and Done. However, it can be more detailed based on your project needs, with added stages like *Analysis, Design, Develop, Test, Review*.

Walking the board involves discussing items currently In Progress, especially those closest to being Done. The team can identify any obstacles or blockers that may be impeding these items' completion and strategize on how best to overcome them.

The Daily Scrum is not a Status Meeting

As teams navigate through the daily Scrum and board-walking activities, it's essential to remember that the Daily Scrum isn't a status meeting. Its primary purpose is to synchronize the team's efforts, not to scrutinize individual team members' work status. It should be a cooperative and transparent platform, where everyone collaborates towards achieving the Sprint goal.

CHAPTER FOUR: FINE-TUNING!

Back at his company, Billy embarked on the journey of transforming his team. He shared his insights from the encounter with the sage and stressed the importance of the Agile mindset. They started to see Agile as more than Scrum and Kanban. They began to question their methods and processes, striving for continuous improvement and growth.

Walking the Board

Billy introduced his team to the concept of walking the board. This practice involved daily stand-up meetings where the team reviewed their progress and planned their work for the day. These meetings encouraged team collaboration, improved communication, and gave everyone a clear picture of the project's status.

Billy enrolled in coaching with Pip beyond the conference to further clarify aspects of Scrum and Agile that stumped him still. His next mentoring session touched on the following concepts:

The Essence of Backlog Refinement

Backlog refinement, previously referred to as backlog grooming, is a crucial practice in Agile development. It involves continuously updating, prioritizing, and breaking down user stories in the backlog to ensure they're clear, relevant, and ready for development in upcoming sprints. It's an opportunity for team collaboration and shared understanding. While it's a task primarily done by the product owner, the insights from the development team can provide valuable context and understanding, thereby aiding in refining user stories.

The Potentially Shippable Increment

An essential output of every Sprint in Scrum is a Potentially Shippable Increment (PSI). This term represents a version of the product that is functional, tested, and potentially ready for delivery to end-users. However, before declaring an increment as potentially shippable, it must meet the team's Definition of Done (DoD).

Definition of Done

The Definition of Done outlines the set of conditions that must be satisfied before the product increment can be considered *done*. It's unique to each team and can include things like completion of testing, completion of documentation, and acceptance criteria for all stories associated with the increment, among other conditions.

Understanding Acceptance Criteria

Acceptance criteria are pivotal in Agile. They define the

specific criteria that a user story must meet to be accepted as complete. These criteria form a critical part of the definition of the user story, guiding developers to meet the exact requests or requirements and providing a clear understanding of when the story can be deemed complete.

Acceptance Criteria vs. Definition of Done

In the Agile world, there's a distinct difference between the acceptance criteria and the Definition of Done. While they both serve to clarify what completion looks like, their application differs significantly.

Acceptance criteria apply to individual user stories. They detail the specific criteria that must be met for the story to be considered done. On the other hand, the Definition of Done is a comprehensive checklist that applies to the entire increment, ensuring it's ready for potential shipping.

Given-When-Then

Given-When-Then is a format commonly used in Agile

development to define acceptance criteria for user stories or features. It provides a structured approach to describe the desired behavior and expected outcomes of a particular functionality.

In this format, "Given" sets the initial context or preconditions, "When" describes the specific actions or events that occur, and "Then" defines the expected results or outcomes. By breaking down the acceptance criteria into these three components, it becomes easier to understand and communicate the requirements clearly.

Using Given-When-Then helps ensure that the development team and stakeholders have a shared understanding of what needs to be implemented and tested. It provides a common language to describe the expected behaviors, making it easier to verify whether the feature meets the desired specifications. This format also facilitates collaboration among team members and helps in creating more reliable and comprehensive tests.

Given-When-Then Examples

Here are a few examples of acceptance criteria and Given-When-Then scenarios:

1. Acceptance Criteria:

    - The user should be able to create a new account with a unique username and a strong password.

    - The system should send a confirmation email to the user upon successful registration.

    - The user should be able to log in with their registered credentials.

Given-When-Then:

    - Given that the user is on the registration page, When they enter a unique username and a strong password, Then they should be able to create a new account.

    - Given that the user has registered successfully, When they check their email, Then they should receive a confirmation email from the system.

    - Given that the user is on the login page,

When they enter their registered username and password, Then they should be able to log in to their account.

2. Acceptance Criteria:

- The search functionality should allow users to search for products by name, category, and price range.

- The search results should be displayed in a paginated format with 10 products per page.

- Users should be able to sort the search results by relevance, price, or customer rating.

Given-When-Then:

- Given that the user is on the search page, When they enter a product name in the search bar and click the search button, Then the system should display the relevant products matching the search criteria.

- Given that the user is on the search results page, When they navigate to the next page or select a specific page number, Then the system should display the corresponding set of products.

- Given that the user is on the search results page, When they choose to sort the results by price in ascending order, Then the system should display the products in the specified order.

These examples showcase how acceptance criteria define the expected behaviors and functionalities of a feature, while the Given-When-Then scenarios outline the specific conditions, actions, and expected outcomes for testing or development purposes.

Sprint Review and Retrospective

Every Sprint culminates in two crucial events – the Sprint Review and the Sprint Retrospective.

The Sprint Review provides an opportunity for the team to present the increment they've created to stakeholders, gather their feedback, and possibly collect additional user stories or requests. It's an event that fuels the continuous improvement engine of Agile.

On the other hand, the Sprint Retrospective is a team-specific event that encourages reflection on the Sprint process. It's a chance for the team to review their successes and challenges, learn from them, and identify potential improvements for the next Sprint.

CHAPTER FIVE: AGILE CHAMPION

Leadership was ecstatic about Billy's Agile epiphany as the results were crystal clear! Their decision to sponsor Pip's training had paid dividends. The team's efficiency was soaring to new heights. Tasks that used to take weeks were now completed in days. The rate of production had dramatically increased, and the quality of the output was unprecedented. Billy's transformation had inspired his team, and their performance had drastically improved.

The newfound Agile mindset had changed the dynamic of the workplace. The team members were engaged and committed to their work. There was a palpable sense of ownership among them, fostering a culture of continuous learning and improvement. Everyone was excited to come to work, to experiment with new ideas, and to solve problems together. It was a stark contrast from the earlier days.

Billy's journey from misunderstanding Agile to mastering its essence was indeed a revelation. He had debunked the myth that Agile was merely a set of practices and had championed the idea that it was a mindset - a philosophy that guided actions, behaviors, and decisions. He was branded as an Agile champion!

More importantly, Billy had demonstrated that Agile was about creating value, both for the team and for the customers. He had shifted the focus from merely doing work to delivering value. This shift had a profound impact on the team's effectiveness and customer satisfaction.

Leadership saw the transformation in Billy and his team and began discussing plans to implement Agile training across the organization. They wanted everyone to have the same understanding and mindset that Billy's team had developed.

Billy, once an Agile skeptic, had become a beacon of Agile philosophy in the organization. His story served as a reminder that understanding and embodying the true essence of Agile is a journey of continuous learning and growth. It is about building a mindset of adaptability, collaboration, and value creation, which goes beyond any specific method or framework.

Billy's team began to embrace the Kaizen lifestyle, a Japanese philosophy emphasizing continuous improvement. They made small, incremental changes to their practices and processes, leading to significant improvements over time. They sought ways to enhance their efficiency and deliver more value, keeping customer satisfaction at the heart of their endeavors.

In the end, it was clear that Agile was not just about doing work in a certain way; it was a paradigm shift in thinking and acting. This shift, as Billy and his team demonstrated, could lead to extraordinary results and a culture of continuous learning and improvement. Billy's journey had just begun, but the impact of his transformation was already making waves across the organization. And so, the tale of Billy Brag and his Agile transformation serves as a testament to the power of the Agile mindset. mindset

The Agile Mindset in Full Swing

As the team adopted this Agile mindset, they began to see tremendous results. Their efficiency skyrocketed as they collaborated more effectively, swiftly adapted to changes, and continuously sought improvements. Billy's team was no longer just using Agile methodologies; they were living Agile principles. They understood that being Agile was not a destination but a journey, a continuous path of learning and improvement.

The Agile Success Story

Billy Brag's story serves as an example for many teams struggling to truly embrace Agile. His transformation from a practitioner of Agile methodologies to a propagator of the Agile mindset is an inspiration for others. Agility, at its core, is about a mindset of continuous growth, learning, adaptability, and collaboration. Remember, Agile is not just about doing Scrum or Kanban; it's about living the Agile principles every day.

CHAPTER SIX: KEY LESSONS LEARNED

This Agile journey has provided you with a comprehensive understanding of the Agile mindset, from its core principles to the specific practices in the Scrum framework. However, it's important to remember that Agile is a flexible approach, and its practices should be adapted to fit the unique needs and circumstances of each team and project. As your team continues to grow and evolve, so too should your application of Agile.

Beyond the Agile Basics

This book has given you a solid foundation in Agile and Scrum, but there's still much to explore in the Agile universe. From advanced Scrum techniques to other Agile frameworks like Kanban and Lean, the Agile world is full of possibilities for further learning and growth. Remember, the journey to Agile mastery is a continuous one, filled with ongoing learning and improvement.

Epilogue: Your Agile Future

As you continue your Agile journey, remember the core values and principles that form the foundation of Agile. Embrace change, foster collaboration, prioritize customer value, and strive for continuous improvement. Keep these principles at the heart of your work, and you'll be well on your way to mastering the Agile mindset.

This concludes our book of Agile and Scrum. Thank you for joining us on this journey, and we wish you all the best in your future Agile endeavors. If you have questions or need further assistance, don't hesitate to reach out.

We hope this book has equipped you with the knowledge and skills to effectively apply Agile principles and practices in your work. Keep learning, keep growing, and keep making strides in your Agile journey. Your Agile future awaits.

Conclusion

Benefits of Agile Adoption

i. Embracing the agile mindset and implementing agile practices can yield numerous benefits for individuals, teams, and organizations:

ii. Adaptability: Agile enables organizations to respond quickly and effectively to changing market conditions, customer needs, and evolving requirements. This adaptability fosters a competitive edge and increases the likelihood of success in dynamic environments.

iii. Increased Customer Satisfaction: By involving customers throughout the development process and delivering working increments of value at regular intervals, agile teams ensure that customer expectations are met or exceeded. This customer-centric approach enhances satisfaction and strengthens relationships.

iv. Faster Time to Market: Agile's iterative and incremental nature allows teams to deliver tangible results more rapidly. By focusing on delivering the most valuable features early on, organizations can gain a competitive advantage by getting their products or services to market faster.

v. Improved Quality: Agile practices, such as continuous integration, frequent testing, and customer feedback loops, contribute to improved product quality. Early and regular testing and feedback help identify and address issues promptly, leading to higher-quality deliverables.

vi. Enhanced Team Morale and Engagement: Agile fosters a collaborative and empowered team environment. By promoting self-organization, shared responsibility, and a focus on delivering value, agile teams experience higher levels of engagement, job satisfaction, and motivation.

Agile is not just a methodology or framework; it is a mindset that drives adaptability, collaboration, and continuous improvement. By understanding and embracing the agile mindset, individuals and teams can navigate the ever-changing landscape of project management and product development more effectively.

Throughout this book, we explored the core principles of agile, the Scrum framework, and the benefits of agile adoption. Remember that agile implementation is a journey, and it requires a commitment to ongoing learning, experimentation, and growth.

Whether you are a project manager, team member, or organizational leader, adopting the agile mindset can lead to more successful and resilient outcomes. Embrace the agile principles, foster collaboration, and be open to change—ultimately, it is the agile mindset that empowers you to thrive in an unpredictable world.'

CHAPTER SEVEN: QUIZ TIME

In this last chapter, we will further explore Agile concepts in a final quiz. Take a best guess (leaving the answer covered with a book mark) and check the answer and close the gaps in your understanding of Agile and Scrum. Remember to visit www.agilemanifesto.org and www.scrumguides.org to download the most current Scrum Guide to close gaps and stay refreshed in all things Scrum and Agile.

Multiple-Choice Questions:

1. What is the primary focus of the Agile Manifesto?

a. Processes and tools

b. Comprehensive documentation

c. Individuals and interactions

d. Contract negotiation

Answer: c. Individuals and interactions

Rationale: The Agile Manifesto emphasizes valuing individuals and interactions over processes and tools.

2. Which framework is commonly used for managing software development projects?

a. Lean

b. Six Sigma

c. Scrum

d. Kanban

Answer: c. Scrum

Rationale: Scrum is a popular framework used for managing software development projects and is based on Agile principles.

3. What is the recommended duration for a Scrum sprint?

a. 1 week

b. 3 weeks

c. 4 weeks

d. It can vary, but should be consistent within a team or project

Answer: d. It can vary, but should be consistent within a team or project.

Rationale: The duration of a Scrum sprint can vary depending on the team or project, but it should remain consistent throughout the project to maintain a predictable cadence. The Scrum guide states 4 weeks or less.

4. **Which role is responsible for removing obstacles and facilitating the progress of the Scrum team?**

a. Scrum Master

b. Product Owner

c. Development Team

d. Stakeholder

Answer: a. Scrum Master

Rationale: The Scrum Master is responsible for removing obstacles and ensuring the Scrum team can work efficiently and effectively.

5. **What is the purpose of a daily Scrum or stand-up meeting?**

a. Status reporting and percent complete

b. Problem-solving and trouble-shooting

c. Synching up & planning

d. None of the above

Answer: d. All of the above

Rationale: The daily Scrum or stand-up meeting serves multiple purposes, but it is not for statusing or solving problems. With work-state transparency, the need for statusing goes away. Infact, giving status in a daily scrum is an anti-pattern. Problems could be raised in a daily scrum. We call these impediments and their resolution happens outside of the daily scrum.

6. **Which of the following is not one of the four values stated in the Agile Manifesto?**
a) Individuals and interactions over processes and tools
b) Working software over comprehensive documentation
c) Customer collaboration over contract negotiation
d) Following a detailed plan over embracing change

Answer: d) Following a detailed plan over embracing change

7. **What is the primary purpose of a Daily Scrum (Stand-up) meeting?**
a) Status reporting to the Scrum Master
b) Detailed discussion of technical issues
c) Identifying obstacles
d) Determining the duration of the sprint

Answer: c) Identifying obstacles

8. **Which role is responsible for prioritizing the product backlog and ensuring it represents the stakeholders' needs?**

a) Scrum Master

b) Development Team

c) Product Owner

d) Project Manager

Answer: c) Product Owner

The Product Owner is accountable for the prioritization of the Product Backlog.

9. **In Scrum, who is responsible for tracking and communicating the progress of the project?**

a) Business Analyst

b) Product Owner

c) Scrum Team

d) Stakeholders

Answer: a) Scrum Team

This is a collective responsibility in Scrum. "Scrum Team" refers to all roles in Scrum. It is not a centralized responsibility around just one person or role.

10. **Which statement best describes the purpose of a sprint review?**

a) To discuss and plan the upcoming sprints

b) To showcase completed work to stakeholders and gather feedback

c) To review and evaluate team member performance

d) To discuss and resolve conflicts within the team

Answer: b) To showcase completed work to stakeholders and gather feedback

11. **During a sprint, the Development Team realizes that the scope of a user story is too large to be completed within the sprint time frame. What should the team do?**

a) Divide the user story into smaller, more manageable tasks for implementation.

b) Inform the Product Owner and negotiate to remove the user story from the sprint backlog.

c) Extend the sprint duration to accommodate the completion of the user story.

d) Delay the start of the next sprint until the user story is completed.

Answer: a) Divide the user story into smaller, more manageable tasks for implementation.

12. **The Product Owner receives a change request from a key stakeholder that would significantly impact the current sprint. What should the Product Owner do?**

a) Accept the change request and incorporate it into the current sprint.

b) Decline the change request and inform the stakeholder that it will be considered in future sprints.

c) Discuss the change request with the Development Team and evaluate its feasibility and impact on sprint goals.

d) Ignore the change request and proceed with the sprint as planned.

Answer: c) Discuss the change request with the Development Team and evaluate its feasibility and impact on sprint goals. Ideally we would like to discourage stakeholders from attempting to modify the Sprint Backlog once the Sprint has commenced. Remember the team has already committed to getting a specific amount of work done. Making unplanned adjustments could significantly alter the Sprint outcome. The Product Owner needs to decide ultimately when a Sprint Backlog should be modified.

13. **A team is trying to determine the best way to prioritize work. Which of the following should they prioritize?**

a. Project management processes

b. Contract negotiation

c. Processes and plans

d. Working software

Answer: d. Working software

Rationale: This is based on the Agile Manifesto principle of "Working software over comprehensive documentation." Agile teams prioritize delivering a working product incrementally, rather than creating extensive documentation.

14. A team is trying to determine the best way to prioritize stakeholder needs. Which of the following should they prioritize?

a. Customer satisfaction

b. Contract negotiation

c. Individual inspiration

d. Following a plan

Answer: a. Customer satisfaction

Rationale: This is based on the Agile Manifesto principle of "Our highest priority is to satisfy the customer." Agile teams prioritize collaboration with the customer, rather than negotiating a formal agreement.

15. A team is trying to balance the need for management control with the need for innovation. Which of the following should they prioritize?

a. Innovation

b. Processes and tools

c. Detailed documentation

d. Management control

Answer: a. Innovation

Rationale: This is based on the Agile Manifesto principle of " The best architectures, requirements, and designs emerge from self-organizing teams." Agile teams prioritize innovation, rather than following strict management control. Remember the choice is only between 2 things.

16. **A team is trying to balance the need for predictability with the need for creativity. Which of the following should they prioritize?**

a. Responding to change

b. Strict adherence to a schedule

c. Predetermined outcomes

d. Interpersonal relationships

Answer: a. Responding to change

Rationale: This is based on the Agile Manifesto principle of "Responding to change over following a plan." Agile teams prioritize being flexible and adapting to changes in requirements, rather than rigidly adhering to a predetermined plan. Even though interpersonal relationships are important, the question is looking for which variable of two to prioritize. The closest option to this scenario is "responding to change."

17. **Fairouz and Jen are working on a software project for Team ITSAGO. They are struggling with managing conflicting priorities between stakeholders. Which of the following should they prioritize?**

a. Stakeholder management

b. Meeting deadlines

c. Technical excellence

d. Customer collaboration

Answer: d. Customer collaboration

Rationale: This is based on the Agile Manifesto principle of "Customer collaboration over contract negotiation." Team ITSAGO should prioritize working closely with the customer to understand their needs and deliver a product that meets those needs, rather than focusing on meeting deadlines or achieving technical excellence. How would the customer feel if they were ignored at the expense of the team's personal standards?

18. **Uche and Shouna are leading a sprint review for Team ITSAGO. They are trying to determine the best way to gather feedback from stakeholders. Which of the following should they prioritize?**

a. Formal feedback processes

b. Customer collaboration

c. Surveys and questionnaires

d. Contract negotiation

Answer: b. Customer collaboration

Rationale: This is based on the Agile Manifesto principle of "Customer collaboration over contract negotiation." Team ITSAGO should prioritize engaging in direct, ongoing communication with stakeholders to gather feedback and improve the product, rather than relying on formal processes or surveys.

19. **Stacy and Ahndrika are working on a feature for Team ITSAGO. They are struggling with how much documentation is necessary. Which of the following should they prioritize?**

a. Comprehensive documentation

b. Working software

c. Following a plan

d. Adherence to the timebox

Answer: b. Working software

Rationale: This is based on the Agile Manifesto principle of "Working software over comprehensive documentation." Team ITSAGO should prioritize delivering a working product incrementally, rather than creating extensive documentation.

20. **Phill and Ahmad are leading a sprint planning meeting for Team ITSAGO. They are trying to balance the need for predictability with the need**

for adaptability. Which of the following should they prioritize?

a. Strict adherence to a schedule

b. Adaptability

c. Uncertainty

d. Complexity

Answer: b. Adaptability

Rationale: This is based on the Agile Manifesto principle of "Responding to change over following a plan." Team ITSAGO should prioritize being flexible and adapting to changes in requirements, rather than rigidly adhering to a predetermined plan.

21. **Stacy and Ahndrika are leading a sprint retrospective for Team ITSAGO. They are trying to determine how to improve the team's performance. Which of the following should they prioritize?**

a. Continuous improvement

b. Meeting deadlines

c. Technical excellence

d. Stakeholder satisfaction

Answer: a. Continuous improvement

Rationale: This is based on the Agile Manifesto principles of" At regular intervals, the team reflects on how to become more effective, then tunes and adjusts its behavior accordingly." It is also based on the principle that states "Continuous attention to technical excellence and good design enhances agility." Team ITSAGO should prioritize continuously improving the team's performance and technical skills, rather than just meeting deadlines or satisfying stakeholders.

22. **Mark and Korvin are working on a new feature for Team PRAIZION. They are trying to balance the need for speed with the need for quality. Which of the following should they prioritize?**

a. Speed

b. Quality

c. Cost

d. Customer satisfaction

Answer: b. Quality

Rationale: In Scrum, the focus should always be on delivering high-quality software. This is because high-quality software is more likely to meet the needs of the customer and be sustainable in the long run. Speed and cost are secondary concerns.

True or False Questions:

23. **True or False: The Agile Manifesto values comprehensive documentation over working software.**

Answer: False

Rationale: The Agile Manifesto values working software over comprehensive documentation.

24. True or False: Scrum teams are self-organizing and cross-functional.

Answer: True

Rationale: Scrum teams are responsible for organizing and managing their own work, and they comprise individuals with different skills and expertise.

25. True or False: The Scrum Master is a hierarchical position that manages the team.

Answer: False

Rationale: The Scrum Master serves as a servant-leader and facilitator for the team, rather than a traditional manager.

26. True or False: User Stories are detailed, technical specifications.

Answer: False

Rationale: User Stories are brief, high-level descriptions of desired features or functionality from the end user's perspective.

27. True or False: Velocity is a measure of the amount of work a Scrum team can complete in a sprint.

Answer: True

Rationale: Velocity represents the total number of story points or work items a Scrum team can deliver within a sprint.

28. The Product Goal a commitment contained in the Sprint backlog. True or False?

Answer: False.

Rationale: The Product Goal is a high-level objective that guides the overall direction and focus of the product. It is not a specific commitment within a Sprint backlog.

29. The Product Owner is a member of the Scrum Team. True or False?

Answer: True.

Rationale: The Product Owner is indeed a member of the Scrum Team. The Scrum Team consists of the Product Owner, the Developers, and the Scrum Master. The Product Owner represents the stakeholders and is responsible for maximizing the value of the product.

30. The product roadmap is created by the Scrum Master and Product Owner. True or False?

Answer: False.

Rationale: The product roadmap is not created solely by the Scrum Master and Product Owner. It is a strategic document that outlines the long-term vision and goals for the product, typically created collaboratively with input from various stakeholders.

31. Stakeholders accept or reject the PSI in the Sprint Retrospective meeting, True or False?

Answer: False.

Rationale: The project stakeholders do not accept or reject the PSI (Potentially Shippable Increment) in the Sprint Retrospective meeting. Acceptance or rejection of the PSI typically happens in the Sprint Review meeting, where stakeholders provide feedback on the delivered increment.

32. The Scrum Master can delegate tasks to team members. True or False?

Answer: False.

Rationale: The Scrum Master does not delegate tasks to team members. The Scrum Master is a servant-leader and facilitator, responsible for ensuring that the Scrum Team follows Scrum principles and practices. Task delegation is typically handled by the Development Team members themselves.

33. The Scrum Master is also known as the Assistant Product Owner. True or False?

Answer: False.

Rationale: The Scrum Master is not known as the Assistant Product Owner. The Scrum Master and the Product Owner have distinct roles and responsibilities within the Scrum Team. The Scrum Master focuses on facilitating the Scrum process and supporting the team, while the Product Owner is responsible for the product vision, backlog management, and maximizing value.

34. The Scrum Team has the power to cancel a troubled sprint. True or False?

Answer: False.

Rationale: The Scrum Team does not have the power to unilaterally cancel a troubled sprint. The decision to cancel a sprint is typically made by the Product Owner in consultation with the Scrum Master and the Development Team. It is a significant decision that should be taken based on careful evaluation and consideration of the situation.

35. True or False: The Definition of Done (DoD) should be determined by the Product Owner.

Answer: False.

Rationale: The Definition of Done is a shared agreement within the Scrum Team, ensuring that the Increment is potentially releasable and meets quality standards. If the Definition of Done for an increment is part of the standards of the organization, all Scrum Teams must follow it as a minimum. If it is not an organizational standard, the Scrum Team must create a Definition of Done appropriate for the product.

36. True or False: The Definition of Ready (DoR) is an optional aspect in Scrum.

Answer: True.

Rationale: The Definition of Ready is not a mandatory aspect in Scrum but can be beneficial to ensure that backlog items are adequately prepared for development.

37. **True or False: The Norming stage in team development is characterized by conflicts and differences among team members.**

Answer: False.

Rationale: The Norming stage is characterized by increased collaboration, harmony, and mutual support as team members establish norms and work well together.

38. **True or False: The Product Backlog is a Scrum artifact that contains only user stories.**

Answer: False.

Rationale: The Product Backlog can contain various types of items, including user stories, technical debt, bugs, and other work items necessary for product development.

39. **True or False: The Scrum Master is responsible for ensuring the Development Team follows the Definition of Done.**

Answer: True.

Rationale: The Scrum Master plays a crucial role in ensuring that the Development Team understands and adheres to the Definition of Done to maintain consistent quality standards.

40. **True or False: The Performing stage in team development is the final stage in the team's evolution.**

Answer: False.

Rationale: The Performing stage is not the final stage but rather the stage where the team reaches its peak performance. The subsequent stage is Adjourning, where the team disbands or transitions.

41. **True or False: The Sprint Goal is created by the Product Owner before the Sprint Planning meeting.**

Answer: False.

Rationale: The Sprint Goal is a collaborative effort between the Product Owner and the Development Team and is typically defined during the Sprint Planning meeting. The Product Owner proposes how the product could increase its value and utility in the current Sprint. The whole Scrum Team then collaborates to define a Sprint Goal that communicates why the Sprint is valuable to stakeholders. The Sprint Goal must be finalized prior to the end of Sprint Planning.

42. True or False: The Scrum Master is responsible for removing impediments.

Answer: True.

Rationale: The Scrum Master serves as a facilitator, ensuring that Scrum events run smoothly and removing any impediments that hinder the Development Team's progress.

43. True or False: The Definition of Ready ensures that every product backlog item is estimated and prioritized.

Answer: False.

Rationale: The Definition of Ready focuses on ensuring that backlog items are well-prepared, clear, estimable and actionable, but it does not necessarily involve estimation and prioritization in and of itself.

44. **True or False: The Storming stage in team development is characterized by high productivity and collaboration.**

Answer: False.

Rationale: The Storming stage is characterized by conflicts, power struggles, and challenges as team members establish their roles and address differences.

45. **True or False: The Daily Scrum is the only Scrum event where the Product Owner must attend.**

Answer: False.

Rationale: While the Product Owner is not mandated to attend the Daily Scrum, they are welcome to participate if they find it valuable. The Product Owner must attend the Sprint Review, Sprint Retrospective and Sprint Planning events.

46. True or False: The DoD is a fixed and unchangeable set of criteria throughout the project.

Answer: False.

Rationale: The DoD can evolve and improve over time as the team learns and adapts. It should be regularly reviewed and updated to reflect the changing needs and goals of the project.

47. True or False: The Forming stage in team development is characterized by uncertainty, politeness, and cautious behavior.

Answer: True.

Rationale: The Forming stage is the initial stage in team development where team members are getting acquainted, establishing their roles, and being polite and cautious in their interactions as they navigate uncertainty.

48. True or False: The Sprint Backlog is created during the Sprint Planning meeting and is fixed without changes possible for the duration of the Sprint.

Answer: False.

Rationale: The Sprint Backlog is created during the Sprint Planning meeting but can be updated and adjusted throughout the Sprint as new information emerges or priorities change.

49. **True or False: The Scrum Master is responsible for assigning tasks to individual Development Team members.**

Answer: False.

Rationale: The Scrum Master is not responsible for assigning tasks. The Development Team is self-organizing and collaboratively decides how to accomplish the Sprint Backlog items.

50. **True or False: The Adjourning stage in team development is characterized by disbanding or transitioning the team.**

Answer: True.

Rationale: The Adjourning stage, also known as the "mourning" stage, is when the team disbands or transitions to new projects. It involves reflecting on accomplishments and saying goodbye.

Open-Ended Questions for Teams & Individuals
1. What is the difference between Agile and Predictive project management (PMBOK® Guide for example)?
2. Discuss/explain each of the manifesto values. Go round your team if studying in a group.
3. Expand on each value and principle and improve on any values or principles as you see fit.
4. What are the differences between how Agile handles the 10 knowledge areas vs. PMBOK® Guide. Discuss all aspects of traditional project management through an Agile lens (Integration, Scope, Schedule, Cost, Quality, Resources, Communications, Risk, Procurement and Stakeholder Management).
5. In traditional project management, what are the biggest issues leading to project failure, risks and scope creep? How does that translate in Agile?
6. Now that you have learnt Agile concepts, how could you keep a project on track?
7. How does the triple constraint of schedule, cost and scope translate into an Agile environment?

See expanded answers here:
www.projectmanagementdoctor.com/agileanswers

Answers to Open-Ended Questions

1. What is the difference between Agile and Predictive project management (PMBOK® Guide for example)?

Agile:

- Iterative and incremental approach
- Emphasizes adaptability and flexibility
- Values collaboration and customer feedback
- Focuses on delivering value early and frequently
- Welcomes changes throughout the project

Predictive (PMBOK® Guide):

- Linear and sequential approach
- Emphasizes upfront planning and documentation
- Values predictability and control
- Focuses on adhering to a predefined plan
- Attempts to minimize changes once the project begins

2. Discuss/explain each of the manifesto values. Go round your team if studying in a group.

The Agile Manifesto values are:

- Individuals and Interactions over Processes and Tools:
    - Emphasizes the importance of collaboration, teamwork, and effective communication among team members.
- Working Software over Comprehensive Documentation:

- Prioritizes delivering a functional product that meets customer needs over extensive documentation.
- Customer Collaboration over Contract Negotiation:
  - Encourages active involvement of customers and stakeholders throughout the project, fostering feedback and collaboration.
- Responding to Change over Following a Plan:
  - Acknowledges that change is inevitable and encourages flexibility and adaptability to address evolving requirements and market conditions.

3. Expand on each value and principle and improve on any values or principles as you see fit.

Value: Individuals and Interactions over Processes and Tools

- Encourages creating an environment that fosters collaboration, trust, and effective communication among team members.
- Recognizes that people and their interactions drive project success more than relying solely on tools and processes.

Value: Working Software over Comprehensive Documentation

- Focuses on delivering a tangible, functioning product that provides value to the customer, rather than excessive documentation that may not directly contribute to the end result.

- However, it's important to note that documentation necessary for understanding, maintaining, and complying with regulations should still be addressed.

Value: Customer Collaboration over Contract Negotiation

- Emphasizes the importance of involving customers and stakeholders throughout the project to gather feedback, ensure alignment with their needs, and foster a collaborative relationship.
- This value can be extended to include effective engagement with end-users and incorporating user feedback during development.

Value: Responding to Change over Following a Plan

- Recognizes that change is inevitable, and projects should be adaptable to address new information, evolving requirements, and market dynamics.
- However, maintaining a baseline plan and controlling changes within reasonable bounds is still essential for managing scope, resources, and expectations.

4. What are the differences between how Agile handles the 10 knowledge areas vs. PMBOK® Guide? Discuss all aspects of traditional project management through an Agile lens (Integration, Scope, Schedule, Cost, Quality, Resources, Communications, Risk, Procurement, and Stakeholder Management).

Agile Approach:

- Integration: Encourages the team to take ownership of integrating all the project's moving parts. Not just the project manager! Also encourages iterative and incremental integration of deliverables, allowing for frequent testing, feedback, and adjustment.
- Scope: Prioritizes delivering the most valuable features first, embraces change, and adjusts scope based on customer and stakeholder feedback.
- Schedule: Uses time-boxed iterations, such as sprints, to provide regular delivery cadence and incorporates feedback to adjust timelines.
- Cost: Adopts an adaptive approach to manage costs by adjusting scope, prioritizing value, and making informed decisions based on feedback.
- Quality: Ensures quality by incorporating testing and continuous integration throughout the development process.
- Resources: Promotes self-organizing teams that collaborate and decide how best to allocate resources to deliver the work.
- Communications: Emphasizes frequent and transparent communication through face-to-face interactions, collaboration tools, and regular feedback loops.
- Risk: Identifies and manages risks through continuous monitoring, adaptation, and early

identification of risks through continuous monitoring, adaptation, and early identification of potential issues.

- Procurement: Adapts procurement processes to accommodate iterative and incremental delivery, allowing for flexibility in supplier engagement and contract negotiations. For example, a customer may be allowed to swap out scope items of similar size without penalty.
- Stakeholder Management: Actively engages stakeholders throughout the project, seeking their feedback and involvement in decision-making processes.

PMBOK® Guide Approach:

These areas could all be performed in repeated cycles throughout the project.

- Integration: Project manager is solely responsible for Integration. Emphasizes the creation of a comprehensive project management plan and the coordination of various project elements to ensure successful project execution.
- Scope: Focuses on clearly defining project scope upfront and managing changes through a formal change control process.
- Schedule: Develops a detailed project schedule based on a sequential approach, with critical path

analysis and network diagrams to manage timelines.

- Cost: Utilizes detailed cost estimation techniques and closely tracks and manages project expenses against the budget.
- Quality: Implements quality control processes to ensure adherence to defined quality standards and project requirements.
- Resources: Assigns and manages resources based on a predetermined project plan, with a focus on resource allocation and utilization.
- Communications: Establishes formal communication channels and documentation to ensure effective information flow and stakeholder engagement.
- Risk: Identifies and analyzes many risks upfront, develops risk mitigation strategies, and implements risk response plans to manage potential threats.
- Procurement: Follows structured procurement processes, including contract creation, bidding, and supplier selection, to manage external resources.
- Stakeholder Management: Identifies and engages stakeholders, develops stakeholder management plans, and manages stakeholder expectations throughout the project.

5. In traditional project management, what are the biggest issues leading to project failure, risks, and scope creep? How does that translate in Agile?

Traditional Project Management

In traditional project management, common issues leading to project failure, risks, and scope creep include:

- Lack of adaptability: Traditional approaches often struggle to address changing requirements and market dynamics, leading to misalignment with customer needs.
- Insufficient stakeholder involvement: Limited stakeholder engagement can result in misunderstood requirements, unmet expectations, and project delays.
- Inadequate risk management: Traditional methods may not prioritize continuous risk monitoring and timely response, leading to unforeseen challenges and delays.
- Scope creep: Poor scope management can lead to uncontrolled additions and changes to project scope, impacting timelines, resources, and costs.

Agile

In Agile, these issues are addressed differently:

- Adaptability: Agile embraces change and provides a flexible framework to address evolving requirements, allowing for continuous feedback and adjustment.
- Stakeholder involvement: Agile promotes active stakeholder engagement throughout the project,

ensuring alignment and regular feedback to mitigate misunderstandings.

- Risk management: Agile incorporates continuous risk monitoring and adapts quickly to address emerging risks, reducing the likelihood of unforeseen challenges.

- Scope management: Agile employs techniques such as iterative planning, prioritization, and regular feedback loops to manage scope effectively, reducing the impact of scope creep.

6. Now that you have learned Agile concepts, how could you keep a project on track?

To keep a project on track in an Agile environment, you can:

- Prioritize and manage the backlog: Continuously prioritize and refine the project backlog, ensuring that the most valuable items are worked on first.

- Use time-boxed iterations: Implement iterative development cycles, such as sprints, with fixed durations to maintain a regular delivery cadence and manage expectations.

- Encourage collaboration and transparency: Foster open and frequent communication among team members, stakeholders, and customers to ensure everyone is aligned and aware of project progress.

- Embrace self-organization: Empower self-organizing teams to make decisions and allocate resources effectively, promoting ownership and accountability.

- Continuously monitor and adapt: Regularly assess project progress, seek feedback, and adapt plans and strategies accordingly, addressing risks and changes promptly.

- Foster a culture of learning and improvement: Encourage continuous learning, reflection, and improvement within the team. Promote a safe environment where mistakes are viewed as opportunities for growth and where experimentation and innovation are encouraged.

7. How does the triple constraint of schedule, cost, and scope translate into an Agile environment? Answers and rationale on a new line.

In Agile, the triple constraint of schedule, cost, and scope is approached differently:

- Schedule: Agile projects utilize time-boxed iterations, such as sprints, to establish a regular cadence for delivering increments of value. The focus is on maintaining a sustainable pace and delivering the highest-priority items within each iteration. The flexibility to adjust scope allows for adapting to changing timelines while ensuring consistent delivery.

- Cost: Agile projects emphasize value-driven decision-making. By continuously prioritizing and delivering the most valuable features first, teams can manage costs effectively. The iterative and incremental approach allows for regular cost evaluation, budget adjustments, and the ability to reprioritize work based on evolving needs and constraints.

- Scope: Agile projects prioritize delivering the most valuable features to customers early and frequently. The scope is adaptable and evolves throughout the project as new information and feedback emerge. Agile teams engage stakeholders and collaborate to define and refine the scope incrementally, ensuring that it aligns with customer needs and business goals.

The rationale behind these adaptations is that Agile recognizes the inherent uncertainties and changes in projects. Instead of attempting to rigidly control all aspects of the project, Agile provides flexibility and focuses on delivering value, enabling teams to respond to feedback and changing requirements effectively. By embracing adaptability and continuous customer collaboration, Agile teams can navigate the triple constraint while delivering products that better meet customer expectations.

Glossary of Common Agile Terms

1. Acceptance Test-Driven Development (ATDD) - Test criteria created before delivery.
2. Agile - Values and principles for agile practices.
3. Agile Coach - Mentors teams through agile transformation.
4. Agile Life Cycle - Incremental approach to project delivery with frequent releases.
5. Agile Manifesto - Official definition of agile values and principles.
6. Agile Mindset - Way of thinking based on Agile Manifesto.
7. Agile Practitioner (Agilist) - Embraces agile values and collaborates.
8. Agile Principles - Twelve principles of agile project delivery.
9. Agile Unified Process - Simplified approach to developing software using agile techniques.
10. Anti-Pattern - Flawed pattern of work to be avoided.
11. Automated Code Quality Analysis - Testing for bugs and vulnerabilities.
12. Backlog (Product Backlog) - Collaborative list of project requirements.
13. Backlog Refinement - Elaborating project requirements to satisfy customers.
14. Behavior-Driven Development (BDD) - Validation practice using test-first principles.

15. Blended Agile - Combining two or more agile frameworks.
16. Blocker (Impediment) - Hindrance or obstacle to team progress.
17. Broken Comb (Paint Drip) - Person with varying skill sets.
18. Burndown Chart - Graphical representation of remaining work in a timebox.
19. Burnup Chart - Graphical representation of completed work toward release.
20. Business Requirement Documents (BRD) - Listing of project requirements.
21. Cadence - Rhythm of execution, also known as a timebox.
22. Collective Code Ownership - Any team member can modify work products.
23. Continuous Delivery - Delivering feature increments immediately to customers.
24. Continuous Integration - Frequently integrating and validating team work products.
25. Cross-Functional Team - Team with all skills for valuable product increments.
26. Crystal Family of Methodologies - Agile methods for adaptability.
27. Daily Scrum (Daily Standup) - Brief daily collaboration meeting.
28. Definition of Done (DoD) - Checklist for customer-ready deliverables.
29. Definition of Ready (DoR) - Checklist for user-centric requirements.

30. DevOps - Practices improving development and operations staff collaboration.
31. Disciplined Agile (DA) - Incremental and iterative solution delivery.
32. Dynamic Systems Development Method (DSDM) - Agile project delivery framework.
33. eXtreme Programming (XP) - Agile software development method.
34. Feature-Driven Development (FDD) - Agile method driven by feature value.
35. Fit for Purpose - Product suitable for its intended purpose.
36. Fit for Use - Product currently usable for its intended purpose.
37. Impediment (Blocker) - Obstacle to team objectives.
38. Increment - Functional, tested, and accepted deliverable.
39. Incremental Life Cycle - Approach providing immediate use deliverables.
40. Information Radiator - Visible display for organization knowledge sharing.
41. I-shaped - Person with single area of specialization.
42. Iteration - Timeboxed cycle of development for product deliverables.
43. Iterative Life Cycle - Approach allowing feedback for unfinished work.
44. Kaizen Events - Collaborative events to improve the system.
45. Kanban Board - Visualization tool to improve workflow efficiency.

46. Kanban Method - Agile method for knowledge work using visual management.
47. Large Scale Scrum (LeSS) - Scrum framework for large product development.
48. Lean Software Development (LSD) - Applying lean principles to software development.
49. Life Cycle - Process of imagining, creating, and using a product.
50. Mobbing - Simultaneous focus by multiple team members on work.
51. Organizational Change Management - Structured approach to transition organizations.
52. Paint-Drip (Broken Comb) - Person with varied skills across specializations.
53. Pair Work (Pair Programming) - Two team members work simultaneously on tasks.
54. Personas - Archetype user with goals, motivations, and characteristics.
55. Pivot - Planned course correction to test new hypotheses.
56. Plan-Do-Check-Act (PDCA) - Iterative method for process control and improvement.
57. Plan-Driven Approach (Predictive Approach) - Traditional work management approach.
58. Predictive Life Cycle - Traditional sequential approach to work management.
59. Project Management Office (PMO) - Management structure for project governance.
60. Product Backlog - List of user-centric requirements for a product.

61. Product Owner (Service Request Manager) - Person responsible for maximizing product value.
62. Progressive Elaboration - Iterative process of increasing plan detail.
63. Release Planning - Collaborative planning of a product release.
64. Retrospective Prime Directive - Guiding principle for retrospective meetings.
65. Scaled Professional Scrum (SPS) - Framework for Scrum in complex environments.
66. Scrum of Scrums - Technique for scaling Scrum to multiple teams.
67. Scrum Team - Combination of team roles in Scrum.
68. Self-Organizing Team - Cross-functional team with fluid leadership.
69. Servant Leadership - Leading through service to team members.
70. Service Request Manager - Person responsible for ordering service requests.
71. Siloed Organization - Organization structured to contribute a subset of required aspects.
72. Smoke Testing - Lightweight testing for important system functions.
73. Specification by Example (SBE) - Collaborative approach to defining requirements.
74. Spike - Short time interval for research or prototyping.
75. Sprint - Timeboxed iteration in Scrum.
76. Sprint Backlog - List of work items for a Scrum sprint.
77. Sprint Planning - Collaborative planning for a Scrum sprint.

78. Story Point - Unit-less measure for relative estimation.
79. Swarming - Collective focus on resolving a specific impediment.
80. Technical Debt - Deferred cost of unfinished work when cutting corners.
81. Test-Driven Development - Defining tests before work for continuous validation.
82. Timebox - Fixed period of time for work.
83. T-shaped - Person with deep specialization and broad abilities.
84. User Story - Brief description of deliverable value for a specific user.
85. User Story Mapping - Visual practice for organizing high-value features.
86. UX Design - Improving product usability and accessibility for better user experience.
87. Value Stream - Organizational construct focused on delivering value to customers.
88. Value Stream Mapping - Lean technique to analyze and improve product/service flow.

About the Author

Phill C. Akinwale, PMP has managed operational endeavors, projects and project controls across government and private sectors in various companies, including Motorola, Honeywell, Emerson, Skillsoft, Citigroup, Iron Mountain, Brown and Caldwell, US Airways and CVS Caremark. With his extensive experience in various facets of Project Management and rigorous project controls, he has trained project management worldwide (NASA, FBI, USAF, USACE, US Army, Department of Transport) across five PMBOK® Guide editions over the last 15 years.

He holds twelve project management certifications with six in Agile Project Management (CSM, PMI-ACP, PSM, PSPO, PAL, SPS). As a John Maxwell Certified Coach and Speaker, Phill delivers workshops, seminars, keynote speaking, and coaching in leadership and soft skills. Working together with you and your team or organization, he will guide you in the desired direction and equip you to reach your goals. Books he has authored include: The No-Good Leader, Earned Value Basics and Project Management Mid-Level to C-Level.

www.ingramcontent.com/pod-product-compliance
Lightning Source LLC
Chambersburg PA
CBHW071114210326
41519CB00020B/6296